SING TO THE LORD A NEW (COVENANT) SONG

SING TO THE LORD A NEW (COVENANT) SONG:

Thinking about the Songs We Sing To God

------------♪------------

Brian V. Janssen

RESOURCE *Publications* • Eugene, Oregon

SING TO THE LORD A NEW (COVENANT) SONG

Copyright © 2010 Brian V. Janssen. All rights reserved. Except for brief quotations in critical publications or reviews, no part of this book may be reproduced in any manner without prior written permission from the publisher. Write: Permissions, Wipf and Stock, 199 W. 8th Ave., Eugene, OR 97401.

ISBN 13: 978-1-60899-016-0

www.wipfandstock.com

Manufactured in the U.S.A.

Unless otherwise noted, Scriptures quotations are from The Holy Bible, English Standard Version, copyright © 2001 by Crossway Bibles, a division of Good News Publishers. Used by permission. All rights reserved.

Lovely Lord
Words and Music by Robert Hartman
Copyright (c) 1997 MPCA Songs of Lehsem
Administered by MPCA Music, LLC
International Copyright Secured All Rights Reserved

TABLE OF CONTENTS

Introduction
The Need for Worship Music Evaluation......................1

Chapter One
Basics of Christian Worship..5

Chapter Two
The Purpose of Music in Worship 11

Chapter Three
Evaluating Worship Music (Part One: The Song's Words)...15

Chapter Four
Evaluating Worship Music (Part Two: The Song's Music)...27

APPENDIX A
Worship Music Evaluation Form 31

Foreword

Like the author of this booklet, I have had the privilege of taking Doctor of Ministry classes at Covenant Theological Seminary. I completed my degree in 1999 with the writing and defense of my dissertation on "A Biblical, Historical, and Contemporary Look at the Regulative Principle of Worship." I now have the privilege of being the instructor of the worship class for the Doctor of Ministry program at the seminary as well as the required Christian Worship class for the Master of Divinity students.

In August of 2002 Brian Janssen was a student in the worship class I taught in Birmingham, Alabama. His class contributions in both the discussions and in his written work were outstanding. The final paper he wrote for the class is essentially what you now have before you in this booklet. His paper was one of the very best ones I have ever received. It articulates a clear biblical foundation informed by church history with wonderful and immediate application into the life of the church.

The "Worship Music Evaluation Form" at the end of this booklet is the best tool I know of to help pastors, worship leaders, and musicians sort through the growing number of songs proposed for Christian worship today as well as the significant number of hymns written throughout the history of the church. I distribute it to all of my classes with my recommendation for them to use it now and throughout their future ministries.

This music evaluation tool is effectively explained in "Sing to the Lord a New Covenant Song." Brian's desire is to choose songs for worship that have content faithful to the Bible in a God-centered and God-directed way. He also longs to see songs in worship help form Christian character and Christian community. Additionally, Brian wants to promote musical expressions of such content that match and help carry the content with excellence and singability along with variety and relevance to the worshiper.

May God use this excellent resource to help his church sing songs in worship that glorify God and edify his people drawing on the richness of the past and the freshness of the present as well as from the world-wide body of Christ past and present.

Dr. Mark L. Dalbey
Covenant Theological Seminary

INTRODUCTION

There has been no element of the recent and regrettable "worship wars" that has led to more controversy and division than that of music. The conversation encompasses not only the proper use of instruments in worship, but the various styles of music in worship. Undoubtedly the conflict was inevitable since music is one of the most powerful carriers of culture. One Christian leader declared: "I don't mind who writes the theological books, so long as I can write the hymns!" Along with the musical revolutions in popular culture have come similar upheavals in church music.

THE NEED FOR WORSHIP MUSIC EVALUATION

Four anecdotes illustrate the need for the church to think carefully about the music we use in worshipping God and to create a tool for evaluating worship music according to the theology we profess.

One occurred in my first year as pastor, over twenty years ago. After a morning worship service an older woman approached me and asked, "Why don't we sing any of the 'good old songs'?" I thought about the hymns we had sung that day. All of them were at least 200 years old. One was written by Bernard of Clairvaux over 800 years ago, so I knew that "good old songs" did not refer to their antiquity. I asked her to prepare a list of songs she preferred as "good old songs." As I suspected, the "good old songs" were those which had been popular when she was a young person, the more subjective revivalist songs of the late 1800s and early 1900s.

A second instance highlighting our need for serious consideration of worship music came during a choir rehearsal. For a few weeks we had been practicing a song titled, "*Was I Faithful?*" I had been concentrating on the tenor part, not paying much attention to the words. But the message of the song seemed somehow problematic. It was based on Jesus' words in Matthew 25:31-40.

> When the King comes in His glory
> and sits upon His throne,
> when nations are gathered around Him,
> and before Him I stand alone;
> my mind searches back through a lifetime
> as I gaze upon the One
> who will grant my right to enter,
> will I hear Him say, "Well done"?
>
> Was I faithful, did I hear their hurting cry,
> did I pass their sorrows by, was I faithful?
> Was I faithful, did I help the blind and weak,
> did my love include the meek, was I faithful?
>
> When on the road as I traveled,
> did I bind up the wounds
> of those who fell astray,
> did I brush their tears away?
> Lord, when my shelter covered me,
> Lord, did my eyes the homeless see;
> did I share with one their need,
> did I share with word or deed,
> Lord, when the hungry needed food,
> Lord did my table do them good,
> was I faithful?
>
> Those who sit at Your right hand
> will hear Your words in deep humility,
> "As you did it unto these, you have done it unto me." [1]

---

[1] Carolyn Hamlin, (Dayton, Ohio: Lorenz Publishing Company, 1998). Used by permission.

The message is appalling. It is Law with no Gospel. One earns the right to enter glory on the basis of one's faithfulness in helping the needy. If those who actually make it to glory have earned their way by their adequate faithfulness, then why should those who sit at Christ's right hand hear his words of welcome "in deep humility"? No humility is required if one has rightly paid one's own way. The words of this anthem are sub-Christian, dangerous to the faith.

A third example illustrates the need to think carefully about worship music. A young man had professed faith in Christ and joined the church. He became devoted to contemporary Christian music, and asked if we could sing his songs in our morning worship. I reminded him that we did sing newer songs accompanied with guitar especially in our evening worship hour. We discussed the lyrics of some of the songs he was suggesting. When I pointed out the theological errors, extreme subjectivism and self-centeredness, he seemed unconcerned. "Does every song have to be theologically correct?" he asked. Unfortunately, this young man became more and more polarized. He declared, "I don't sing hymns." In morning worship, he refused to open a hymnal and stared at the front of the sanctuary during congregational singing. Later, he approached the worship committee and asked that we replace hymns with the congregation singing along to pre-recorded CD's. Eventually he left the church.

In a fourth instance, a woman not in our congregation excitedly told me of a song another church had sung the previous Sunday morning. The song is well-known, written by Gary Oliver, and is entirely composed of the repeated words "celebrate" and Jesus" along with an affirmation of Jesus' resurrection.[2] When I pointed out that the song was theologically vacuous and repetitive and that it teaches nothing substantive about the purpose of the resurrection of Christ which we are suppose to be celebrating, she replied, "Oh, I know, I know. But I like it!"

---

[2] "Celebrate Jesus" by Gary Oliver, Integrity's Hosanna! Music, 1988.

CONCLUSION

It is obvious that in the preceding stories I have made some assumptions already about the purpose of music in worship: that the lyrics should be doctrinally correct and weighty, that they should focus more on God's character and acts (objective) rather than on my feelings (subjective), that the message of worship music should progress and not merely be repetitive, and that people clearly have widely different tastes in music. Before we talk about worship music, then, let's consider some basics of Christian worship.

Chapter One

BASICS OF CHRISTIAN WORSHIP

Before considering worship music, it is helpful to review broader issues and aspects of Christian worship.

Worship as a Covenant Renewal

God's people rightly gather in many ways and for different purposes: small groups, fellowship groups, mission groups, classes, choirs, hymn sings or sing-a-longs, concerts, social issues meetings and rallies, elders' and deacons' meetings, women's meetings, youth meetings, congregational business meetings, etc. But when the whole congregation gathers each week for worship on the Lord's Day as the Lord commands, under the direction of the church officers, it meets for a special purpose. It is a meeting with God, called by God, and directed by God's Word. And since the sign of the New Covenant (the Lord's Supper) is to be celebrated at this meeting (weekly, monthly, quarterly, but at this meeting) this weekly, Lord's Day meeting with God is primarily a New Covenant renewal ceremony. Robert Webber writes:

> Christian worship is like Hebrew worship. In worship God renews his covenant with us. In worship our relationship to God is deepened and strengthened when the order itself represents God's speaking to us and God's saving us through the life, death, and resurrection of his Son. The order brings that ancient event into our experience and causes, by the power

of the Holy Spirit, a meeting to take place between God and us.[3]

Michael Horton observes the connection between worship and the ancient covenant:

> Central to a biblical understanding of worship is the notion of *covenant*. As biblical scholarship has shown in recent decades, the Old Testament is largely in the form of a treaty, with the great king or emperor promising to protect smaller nations that could not generate their own standing army. In exchange, the great king would receive loyalty from his vassals. They would not turn to other kings for security but would uphold the treaty. A covenant always involved three things: a historical prologue that gave the narrative rationale for the covenant, a list of commands and prohibitions, and a list of sanctions—the benefits for those who fulfill the treaty's terms, the penalty for violating them.[4]

In this ceremony, the great King meets with his subjects. The terms of the New Covenant (Law and Gospel) are recalled: its stipulations and requirements and its benefits and penalties (blessings and cursings). The King declares again his salvation, his protection and provision, while the people reaffirm their faith in the King, their loyalty and allegiance and love. And the sign of the New Covenant (the sacrament of the Lord's Supper) is offered and received.

If this is the purpose of corporate worship, then the music we employ must contribute to the renewal of the New Covenant. It must be focused on and honoring to the great King. It must be true to the New Covenant, to the Gospel of God's work for us in Christ. It must accurately reflect both God's holy and perfect Law (and our absolute inability to fulfill it) and Christ's perfect obedience to the Law in our place, his substitutionary death for sinners in our place, and his resurrection to life for us. It must address our response to God through faith, love and obedience (the imperative) always in terms of God's prior greatness and glory, and his gracious work on our behalf (the indicative). Since the covenant is not primarily between God and individuals but

---

[3] Robert Webber, *Worship is a Verb* (Waco, Texas: Word Books, 1985), 130.
[4] Michael Horton, *A Better Way* (Grand Rapids: Baker Books, 2002), 28.

between God and his people, New Covenant music should preferably be corporate (we) rather than personal (I).

Worship as Glorifying God and Strengthening God's People

This covenant renewal/ worship is to an end. John L. Frame indicates such purposes as "glorifying God" and "strengthening the church":

> We might focus on the broadest, most general commands of Scripture, such as "Do it all for the glory of God" (1 Cor. 10:31) and "All of these must be done for the strengthening of the church" (1 Cor. 14:26), and seek to develop the structure of worship out of them. On that basis, we would simply ask, What brings glory to God? and, What brings strengthening (edification) to the church?[5]

Frame goes on to become more specific in delineating the New Testament components of worship, but these twin purposes remain central. Marva Dawn refines these purposes. "Glorifying God" (1 Cor. 10:31) or "God as the center of worship," she specifies as keeping God both the subject and object of worship.

The *subject* of worship is God. It is about God, his glory, greatness and works for us.

> It is absolutely essential that the Church keep God as the subject of worship since to be Christian means to believe that the God revealed in Jesus Christ is everything to us—Creator, Provider, Sustainer; Deliverer, Redeemer, and Lord; Sanctifier, Inspirer and Empowerer. Friendship, instruction, and other aspects of the gathered community are important, but we lose our reason for being if we do not constantly remember that God has called us to be his people and that our ability to respond to that call in worship and life is totally the gift of God's grace.[6]

---

[5] John M. Frame, *Worship in Spirit and Truth* (Phillipsburg, New Jersey: P & R Publishing, 1996), 52.
[6] Marva J. Dawn, *Reaching Out Without Dumbing Down* (Grand Rapids: W. B. Eerdmans

And the *object* of worship is also God. Worship is directed to God, as we respond to his greatness, glory and works for us.

> ...Christian worship is about offerings or sacrifice. Jesus manifested what worship means in his complete act of sacrifice on the cross....The gifts of worship flow from God the subject and return to God the object of our reverence. [7]

She quotes C. Welton Gaddy,

> "Worship is for God. Only! The chief aim of worship is to please God—whether by adoration and praise, prayer and proclamation, confessions and offerings, thanksgivings and commitment, or by all these actions combined." [8]

But how does worship "strengthen" God's people (1 Cor. 14:26)? In two ways. Worship is to form Christian character and form Christian community. She warns against "narcissism" in contemporary worship, and agrees with David F. Wells in his landmark book, *"No Place for Truth,"* that "self-oriented" worship often enjoys immediate but only temporary success.

> Worship practices that only evoke good feelings and thereby foster a character that seeks instant gratification might be enormously successful at first, but the costs, though not immediately obvious, may be high. The very methods that attract crowds might also prevent the development of habits of reflection and learning. A focus on self and feelings limits the nurturing of a godly and outreaching character.[9]

But corporate worship is also intended to form community. When God calls us to Christ, he calls us to his church. God's plan has always been to save a people, and not just individuals. This is the reason why we gather together for worship, why we do not worship at home,

---

Publishing Co., 1995), 76.
[7] Ibid., p. 80.
[8] Ibid.
[9] Ibid., p. 111.

alone, plugged into our cyberchurch monitor or simply watching the worship show on television. God calls us together as his household, his family, as the body of Christ together.

The earliest Christians were often persecuted for their faith in Christ. The easiest way they could be captured and arrested was when they were meeting together, engaging in (illegal) Christian worship. And yet it never occurred to them simply to stay home and worship on their own where they would not be detected and caught. Why? Because they understood that worship was only rightly done in the context of God's people together. Coming together for worship expresses a theological truth: when we belong to Christ, we belong to each other. As a common life is within us, so we must share our common life together. Marva Dawn expresses how worship music can either nourish or disable this sense of community.

> We must be careful in choosing new music from our era (as opposed to the music in hymnbooks, which has already for the most part been sorted by history so that the best usually remains). Since we live in an increasingly narcissistic culture, we must guard against new songs that are self-centered, that fail to convey the we-ness (and wee-ness) of the Church. We want to avoid music that focuses only on our personal feelings of happiness, instead of equipping us to be a missional community that reaches out beyond ourselves with the good news of grace in Christ and cares for the world around us with peacemaking and justice building.[10]

In summary, worship should be about God and directed to God. It should help to form Christian character and foster Christian community.

Worship as a Meeting, Not Performance

Since worship is a called meeting between God and his covenant people for the purpose of renewing the covenant and since worship is to be God-centered, New Covenant-oriented, and leading to Christian

---

[10] Marva J. Dawn, *A Royal "Waste" of Time* (Grand Rapids: W. B. Eerdmans Publishing Co., 1999), 182.

character and community, it is exceedingly unhelpful to speak of worship in terms of a performance.

Is worship a performance? Only if we are performing. But if this is a New Covenant renewal, then who is performing and who is observing? I reject Kierkegaard's (admittedly time-honored) analogy of God as audience, worship leaders as prompters, and congregation as actors.[11] Worship is a meeting between the great King and his delighted, eager people. Indeed, the great drama of redemption is remembered in Word and Sacrament, but God's people are not performing for God. We are meeting with him in joyful gratitude and love. Gifts are certainly exchanged. God offers gifts of grace, strengthening faith and producing the fruit of the Spirit. We offer our gifts of praise, of willing service, of devotion, and of alms for the poor. Even though a choir or musician prepares and practices the gift to be offered so that it is a gift of excellence, yet it is not a performance to be lauded either for the congregation or God. It is a gift offered to the glory of God.

---

[11] Cited by Barry Liesch, *The New Worship* (Grand Rapids: Baker Books, 1996), 123.

Chapter Two

------------♫------------

THE PURPOSE OF MUSIC IN WORSHIP

If worship is a meeting with God in which God renews his covenant with us, why use music? In modern business meetings in which important contracts are developed and signed, the parties do not sing the terms of their agreement to one another. Perhaps worship services should be like official business conferences with fine print, codicils, lawyers, and notaries in abundance. Why sing when we renew our covenant with God?

Music in worship, both vocal (e.g. Psalm 5:11, 7:17, 9:2,11, 13:6, 18:49, 21:13, 27:6, 30:4, 30:12, 32:1, 33:1,3, 47:6, 47:7, 51:14, 57:7,9, 59:16-17, 61:8, 63:7, 66:2, 4, 67:4, 68:4, 32, 71:22-23, 75:9, 81:1, 87:7, 89:1, 89:12, 90:14, 92:4, 95:1, 96:1-2, 12-1313, 98:1, 8-9, 101:1, 104:12, 33, 105:2, 108:1, 3, 119:172, 132:9, 132:16, 135:3, 137:3-4, 138:1, 138:5, 144:9, 145:7, 146:2, 147:1, 7, 149:1, 5) and instrumental including harp, lyre, flute, cymbals, tambourine (e.g. Psalm 33:2, 43:4, 49:4, 57:8, 71:22, 81:2, 92:3, 98:5, 108:2, 144:9, 147:7, 149:3, 150:3-5) is undeniably endorsed and even commanded in Scripture. The purpose of music is not defined but it appears to be an aid in expressing worship, especially supplying beauty and emotion to words of worship.

Our singing to God, indeed all of worship, is to be considered a response to what God has already done for us in Christ. Why do we sing in a church service? Because God is great and has done great things for us. So our singing should rightly center on God and what he has done for us. That is truly worth singing about.

But why *singing*? Why not just speaking? It seems that there is something about worshiping God that requires music as a response of our whole person. Jonathan Edwards writes:

> And the duty of singing praises to God, seems to be appointed wholly to excite and express religious affections. No other reason can be assigned, why we should express ourselves to God in verse, rather than in prose, and do it with music, but only, that such is our nature and frame, that these things have a tendency to move our affections.[12]

Apparently we cannot fully express our worship to God without music. In commenting on 1 Peter 1:8, New Testament scholar Wayne Grudem suggests that one reason we *sing* our praise to God is because our joy in Christ is "inexpressible." "It thus reminds us of the value of singing and other kinds of music in worship, for music often provides a vehicle for expressing the fullness of joy in a Christian's heart in a way that is much more effective than spoken words alone."[13]

Over and over in Scripture we find the pattern: "BECAUSE God is great, or BECAUSE of the great things he has done, I WILL SING PRAISES TO HIM...." Here are some examples from the Psalms:

Psalm 13:6: *"I will sing to the LORD, because he has dealt bountifully with me."*

Psalm 18:48-49: *"[Y]ou exalted me above those who rose against me; you rescued me from the man of violence. For this I will praise you, O LORD, among the nations, and sing to your name."*

Psalm 27:5-6 *"For he will hide me in his shelter in the day of trouble; he will conceal me under the cover of his tent; he will lift me high upon a rock. And now my head shall be lifted up above my enemies all around me, and I will offer in his tent.*

---

[12] Jonathan Edwards, *Religious Affections*. Ed. John E. Smith. (New Haven Conn.: Yale University Press, 1959), p. 115.
[13] Wayne Grudem, 1 Peter: An Introduction and Commentary (TNTC). (Grand Rapids: William B. Eerdmans Publishing Company, 2007), 66.

sacrifices with shouts of joy; I will sing and make melody to the LORD."

The skeptic Mark Twain once said, "Man is the only creature that becomes embarrassed, or that needs to." I would suggest that Christians are the only people who rightly sing, or have good reason to. In fact, the emphasis Paul places on "gratitude" in singing, clearly demonstrates that music in worship is in response to God: *"Let the word of Christ dwell in you richly as you teach and admonish one another with all wisdom, and as you sing psalms, hymns and spiritual songs* **with gratitude in your hearts to God.***"* (Colossians 3:16, emphasis added.)

This means that using music in worship to crank up feelings in people is a mistake. Music is not to create the response; it is to be a part of the response. It is true that certain forms of music can induce various emotional states. So a very loud and vigorous band concert can stimulate a mood of agitation, can raise the pulse, and generate certain feelings. We have all felt that effect. Or certain sad songs can make us feel pensive and reflective, somber and mournful. Our moods can be shaped and influenced simply by the music we hear. But we must be careful: music in worship is not intended to create an artificial response, but to be a part of the response.

Various elements of worship can be sung and not merely spoken. Adoration, praise, thanksgiving, prayers of supplication or confession of sin, ascriptions to God, confessions or creeds, even the Scripture lesson can be sung. We find all of these actions in the biblical Psalms. In more liturgical worship, the various responses are usually memorized and sung by the congregation, while the Psalm or Gospel may be chanted.

Of concern, however is the contemporary notion that music somehow "brings us into God's presence" or is a "spiritually generative event" that "connects us with God." Michael Horton, in reviewing an article in *Worship Leader* which advocates this very understanding of music, asks a penetrating question: "Can music really connect us to God? Not the Word as it is sung but the music itself? In a generation that views music (especially pop music) as the lifeline to selfhood and the world, it is not surprising that it would be regarded as the best bridge to God."[14] We should heed St. Augustine's ancient caution: "So oft as it befalls me to be more moved with the voice of the singer than with the thing sung, I confess myself to have grievously offended: at which time I

---

[14] Horton, *A Better Way*, p. 28.

wish rather not to have heard the music."[15] Edwards reminds us:

> Indeed there may be such means, as may have a tendency to stir up the passions of weak and ignorant persons, and yet have no great tendency to benefit their souls. For though they may have a tendency to excite affections, they may have little or none to excite gracious affections or any affections tending to grace.[16]

Worship music must always be understood as the servant of the words, enhancing the message with beauty and appropriate emotion. Music must never seek to obscure or overwhelm, carry or contradict the message of the words. At the same time it must be admitted that music as an art medium already carries its own message. Music can be dissonant, light, somber, energetic, plodding, ponderous, trite, involved, and so forth, and each of those musical styles must carefully match, assist, and enhance the message of the words. But in the end music must always serve the message and never become the message.

A helpful rule of thumb to determine whether the music serves the message or has *become* the message is to ask if the words of this song can stand on their own. If the words are so banal or weightless that they need a catchy tune or thumping beat to carry them, then the music has probably become the message. What's interesting is that all of the biblical psalms must stand on their words alone, since we do not have any of the tunes that originally accompanied them. If song lyrics have little meaning or power when we only read them, we probably do not need to sing them.

---

[15] Quoted in James D. Robertson, *Minister's Worship Handbook* (Grand Rapids: Baker Book House, 1974) 76.
[16] Edwards, *Religious*, p. 122.

Chapter Three

EVALUATING WORSHIP MUSIC
(PART ONE: THE SONG'S WORDS)

Music to be used in worship should reflect these theological understandings. To that end, I have developed weighted criteria with which to assess songs for worship and placed them into a form (see Appendix A). I have sought to make the evaluation instrument as objective as possible, though complete objectivity would be impossible. The form rates both the words and the music of each song, and each of the specific criteria will be explained below.

Since the song's message is of greater concern than its music, the words of the song are evaluated first. One should always keep in mind that inadequate worship songs can possibly be redeemed by changing inappropriate words, eliminating problematic verses, or adding new, more faithful verses to songs. For example, songs that are individualistic can often be made corporate by changing the pronouns from "I" to "we." Songs that only speak about God can often be addressed to God. Purely subjective songs, those which focus on the response (the imperative) without the basis of God's person and work (the indicative) are more difficult to rescue. Perhaps most of these should perish by attrition, or perhaps whole new verses could be written.

PRELIMINARY CONCERNS

Two preliminary concerns, more foundational than the rest, are addressed first, namely that the words of the song be true, and that the words of the song be specifically Christian.

_____ **1. These words are biblically true (doctrinally correct) in every way. (PASS or FAIL)**

Words we sing to God or about God in worship must be true, that is, they must be in accordance with God's Word. And since our church is Presbyterian and Reformed, the doctrinal content of each song must not contradict Reformed doctrine. Singing to or about God that which is false is nothing less than false worship, i.e. idolatry.

The best way to ensure that worship songs are theologically accurate is to use a denominational hymnal, where the songs have already been screened through the filters of history and the hymnal's editors. In some cases, however, this screening may not have been particularly careful, or may have had other agendas (radical feminism, political correctness, etc.), so this may not be the most helpful criteria.

Again we should note that even untrue songs may be rescued by correction. For example, our hymnal contains a fine hymn which we often use during communion, *"Jesus, Thy Blood and Righteousness,"* written by Nicolaus L. von Zinzendorf and translated by John Wesley. But the last stanza is clearly Arminian:

> Lord, I believe were sinners more
> Than sands upon the ocean shore,
> Thou hast for all a ransom paid,
> For all a full atonement made.[17]

This is easily remedied by omitting the verse (which we always do).

Or a popular song which we sometimes use in worship, *"The Power of Your Love,"* by Geoff Bullock, contains the inaccurate line: "Lord, unveil my eyes, *let me see You face, to face....*"[18] Moses requested this of God and was mercifully denied, since it would have killed him (Exodus 33:20). It is unwise to repeat this request today, since the answer would be the same. So, to rescue this song, we have changed the line to read, "Lord, unveil my eyes, *to the wonder of your grace....*" This is not

---

[17] *The Hymnal for Worship and Celebration*, (Waco, Texas: Word Music, 1986), No. 193.
[18] *Maranatha! Music Praise Hymns and Choruses* (expanded 4th ed.; Laguna Hills: The Corinthian Group, 1997), No. 157.

Chapter 3: Evaluating Worship Music (The Words)

only a wiser request of God, but also reflects how God answered this question for Moses by instead declaring to Moses his grace (see Exodus 34:6-7).

_____ **2. These words are distinctively Christian, either Trinitarian or referencing the atoning work of God in Christ (some mention of grace, mercy, redemption, etc.), or both. For example, it would be awkward to sing this song in a Jewish synagogue. (O.K. or CAUTION)**

New Covenant worship should be specifically Christian. Each worship song should contain some element that is distinctively Christian, either a reference to the Triune nature of God or some mention of God's work in Christ, or both. This would include some word about God's grace, forgiveness, redemption, anything that delineates the basis of our approaching God not on our merits but on God's mercy in Christ.

My first instinct was to make this likewise a "PASS-FAIL" criterion. But that was until I began to assess various hymns according to it and found to my dismay that many beloved hymns of the faith fail to make the grade, while numerous others barely qualify. While fine in other respects, hymns such as *"Immortal, Invisible, God Only Wise," "The Lord's My Shepherd, I'll Not Want," "O God, Our Help in Ages Past,"* and *"I Sing the Mighty Power of God"* would all fail this test, and several others would pass only by the use of a single word such as "mercy," "grace" or "salvation." When worship songs fail to contain this explicitly Christian, redemptive focus, it is vital to ensure that other elements of the worship service compensate.

Next we turn to theological concerns about the purpose of worship, namely that worship is to be about God and to God, and that worship should form Christian character and foster Christian community.

A. THIS SONG IS "ABOUT" GOD
(God as the subject of worship)

_____ **3. These words' subject is about some aspect of God's character or God's works that is developed in a consequential way. (No = 0, Somewhat = 10, Yes = 20)**

At the bare minimum our worship music should at least identify the God whom we profess to worship. Even better, the worship itself should lift up or celebrate some aspect of God's character or work. Therefore, worship music must contain some significant reference to God's identity, person and/or great acts of creation, providential care, redemption, rule, etc. Because of the greater gravity of this concern, it was given more weight than most other criteria.

David F. Wells performed a comparative survey of popular hymns and choruses looking for the presence of significant theological content. He made the following observation with respect to "classical spirituality" (represented by traditional hymns) vs. "postmodern spirituality" (represented by choruses):

> What is so striking about the hymnody—if that is what it is—of this postmodern spirituality, however, is its parasitic nature. It lives off the truth of classical spirituality but frequently leaves that truth unstated as something to be assumed, whereas in the hymnody of the classical spirituality the truth itself is celebrated. The one rejoices in what the other hides.[19]

In his analysis of the most popular chorus books from Vineyard and Maranatha! sources, nearly 60% offered "no doctrinal grounding or explanation for the praise," unlike the Psalms in which the imperative (praise response) is almost always grounded on the indicative (truth about God). Wells explains his method: "The rule I used was that in any of the songs in these two books, the simple repetition of a word that could have doctrinal content would not be counted unless some small elaboration of that word occurred in the context."[20] This would be a wise rule to employ in determining the theological content of songs as a part of this evaluation.

_____ **4. These words evidence a progression of thought, not merely repetition of thought.**
(No = 0, Somewhat = 5, Yes = 10)

Repetition itself is acceptable (note the repetitive refrain of Psalm

---

[19] David F. Wells, *Losing Our Virtue* (Grand Rapids: W. B. Eerdmans Publishing Co., 1998), 44.
[20] Ibid., p. 44, n26.

Chapter 3: Evaluating Worship Music (The Words)

136, for example). Many songs follow the pattern of several stanzas, each followed by the same refrain. Yet in most of these (as in Psalm 136), the refrain is a fresh response to a new truth; there is progression, not stagnation of thought. This is different from singing the same, short verse over and over. Not long ago, I saw on a printed song sheet the words of the song "*Celebrate, Jesus*" mentioned in the introduction above. At the end of the words was a note in parenthesis: "(repeat until euphoric)." This was a strikingly honest admission. Repeating an admittedly repetitive song tends to disengage the mind so the emotions can take over. This is the purpose and effect of the "mantra" of Eastern meditation. The words of the worship song must evidence a progression of thought.

B. THIS SONG IS "TO" GOD
(God as the object of worship)

_____ **5. These words are written with excellence and are a fitting offering to present to God.**
(No = 0, Somewhat = 10, Yes = 20)

Though worship is not a performance for God, in worship we do offer gifts to God, and these gifts should be our best. The words of worship music should evidence "excellence in poetic craftsmanship. If God is infinitely wonderful, we want to choose the best writing available to worship him."[21] This criterion is weighted more heavily by design. Priests who offered God inferior sacrifices in the post-exilic temple showed contempt for God's name. God indicted them:

> When you offer blind animals in sacrifice, is that not evil? And when you offer those that are lame or sick, is that not evil? Present that to your governor; will he accept you or show you favor? says the LORD of hosts. (Malachi 1:8)

One musically engaging chorus we sing in worship is "*Lovely Lord*," by Bob Hartman.

---

[21] Dawn, *A Royal "Waste" of Time*, p. 303.

Sing to the Lord a New (Covenant) Song

1. You are filled with compassion and mercy and grace
With Your banner of love over me
I am longing to see You one day face to face
And to be with You endlessly. Lord, how lovely You are to me

Chorus:
    Lovely Lord, You are all to me
    Lovely Lord, Full of purity
    Worthy of honor and majesty
    Lord, how lovely You are to me

2. You are bright as the sunrise and fairest of all
Unto You all the glory will be
You are God of creation and Lord of my life
I will worship You faithfully. Lord, how lovely You are to me
    (Chorus)

3. We will worship the name of the Holiest One
We will worship Your excellency
We will give You the glory For things You have done
And be thankful eternally. Lord, how lovely You are to me
    (Chorus)[22]

    The song is enjoyable and does contain significant theological truth. But it is not tightly organized. It reflects more a collection of largely unrelated ideas, almost haphazardly tossed together. In the chorus, for example, in the phrase "full of purity," the notion of purity (though true) is undeveloped and absent from the rest of the song (one suspects it was chosen because it rhymes with "me"). The second line of the second verse contains a grammatical error by ending a sentence with an intransitive verb. This is, perhaps, a minor point, but again, one suspects that this was deliberate in order to rhyme with "me." The song is basically true, but does not evidence "excellence in poetic craftsmanship." We will continue to sing it, though I doubt anyone will remember it in a decade or two.

---

[22] *Lovely Lord* by Bob Hartman, (Petsong Music, 1997). Used by permission.

_____ **6. These words, or a portion of these words, are directed to God and not merely about God.**
(No = 0, Somewhat = 5, Yes = 10)

Since worship is a meeting with God and not merely a memorial service for God, it is important that we recognize his presence in worship and address him directly. In this respect, perhaps modern choruses enjoy an advantage over many hymns. For example, my favorite hymn, *"Praise to the Lord, the Almighty"* (Neander/Winkworth) never leaves the third person (except when calling the faithful to worship). Praise is urged to God, but God is never addressed. The well-known *"How Great Thou Art"* (Stuart K. Hine) follows an interesting pattern. It contains four stanzas, all in the third person (about God), and each of these is followed by a refrain in the second person (to God). Many third person hymns and songs can be rescued from this affliction by changing the words, or a portion of the words, to be addressed to God.

C. THIS SONG HELPS FORM CHRISTIAN CHARACTER

Christian character is understood to be God-centered as opposed to self-centered; righteous through faith in Christ's completed work, rather than self-righteous by following the rules; and performing good works as response to God's grace rather than as a meritorious duty. Worship music will help to form this Christian character by pointing to God and celebrating God's goodness and redemptive works in Christ as the basis for the Christian's faithful response.

_____ **7. These words avoid excessive narcissism (self-absorption). They are more about God's work for us (objective) than our work for or feelings about God (subjective). (No = 0, Somewhat = 5, Yes = 10)**

Undoubtedly we live in a self-centered age. In his book, *Psychology as Religion,*[23] psychologist Paul Vitz traces the rise of selfism in American culture during the middle of the twentieth century through the influence of the selfist psychologists (Maslow, Rogers, Jung, etc.). Christopher

---

[23] Paul Vitz, *Psychology as Religion* (Grand Rapids: W. B. Eerdmans Publishing Co., 1977).

Lasch (*The Culture of Narcissism*[24]) describes how the narcissistic personality, which was previously considered a psychological disorder, has now become mainstream and commonplace. Authentic worship recognizes that according to Scripture, the self is not to be esteemed, fulfilled, or actualized but denied (Matthew 16:24), controlled (Galatians 5:23), put off (Ephesians 4:22), and crucified (Romans 6:6).

Unfortunately, much worship music has been written that is selfist, subjective, or both. From *"In the Garden"* to *"I Just Came to Praise the Lord,"* God has been relegated to the back row while my self and my feelings have barged into the spotlight. For example, the index of the expanded 2nd edition of the *Maranatha! Praise Chorus Book* lists 28 songs whose titles or first lines begin with the pronoun "I" and another 16 that begin with the pronoun "we," for a total of 44 songs that tell what I or we feel or will do. Contrast that to 17 which begin with "Jesus," 6 with "Father," 5 with "God," 8 with "He" in reference to God, 15 with "Lord," and 2 with "Spirit" for a total of 53. Though God wins by a narrow margin, the point is that the totals should not nearly be so close.

_____ **8. These words' response of praise, confession, love, etc. (the imperative) is based on relevant and significant truth about God and his works (the indicative).**
(No = 0, Somewhat = 5, Yes = 10)

The indicative (who God is, what God has done) gives rise to the imperative (our response in worship or obedience). This is the regular pattern among the Psalms. For example, Psalm 100 bases the call to worship on the fact of God's worth: "do this" (the imperative), "because of is or does this" (the indicative).

Psalm 100
1. Make a joyful noise to the LORD, all the earth! *(Imperative)*
2. Serve the LORD with gladness! *(Imperative)*
   Come into his presence with singing! *(Imperative)*
3. Know that the LORD, he is God! *(Indicative)*
   It is he who made us, and we are his; *(Indicative)*
   we are his people, and the sheep of his pasture. *(Indicative)*

---

[24] Christopher Lasch, *The Culture of Narcissism* (New York: Norton, 1978).

Chapter 3: Evaluating Worship Music (The Words)

4. Enter his gates with thanksgiving and his courts with praise! *(Imperative)*
   Give thanks to him; praise his name! *(Imperative)*
5. For the LORD is good; his love endures forever, *(Indicative)*
   and his faithfulness to all generations. *(Indicative)*

Some extol the value of modern praise songs because they are commonly based on the Psalms, the very words of God. But often the response or imperative is lifted out of the Psalm while the indicative is left unstated. And, as Michael Horton points out,

> Vagueness about the object of our praise inevitably leads to making our own praise the object. Praise therefore becomes an end in itself, and we are caught up in our own "worship experience" rather than in the God whose character and acts are the only proper focus.[25]

Even the time-honored "*What a Friend We Have in Jesus*" (Joseph M. Scriven) falls into this error. It is almost completely imperative. It does point to Jesus as one who will help with life's problems, but not as the holy sin-bearer and divine Son of God. In fact, it gives us no theological basis for approaching God in prayer, other than Jesus being a faithful friend. It does name him as "Precious Savior" and "Refuge" but fails to define or develop these terms. One might find the same psychological relief from talking to a good therapist or a trusted spouse.

D. THIS SONG FOSTERS CHRISTIAN COMMUNITY

The other way worship is to strengthen (1 Corinthians 14:26) worshippers is through fostering Christian community. Worship leaders must avoid anything that might make worship appear to be the private activity of individuals instead of the corporate act of the people of God. Edith Blumhofer offered this critique of earlier Pentecostalism:

> What was perceived as corporate worship might alternatively be described as simultaneous individual worship. Pentecostals perhaps met together as much to pursue individual experiences

---

[25] Horton, *A Better Way*, p. 26.

as to express corporate solidarity as the people of God.[26]

This image haunts me: individual worshippers sitting or standing together yet pursuing individual experiences, worshippers who only (accidentally) happen to be occupying the same room. It is utterly inimical, foreign, and destructive to the body of Christ. Yet this is not only true of Pentecostals. Much "Praise and Worship" styled worship tends toward the individualist's experience. The music of corporate worship should require more than one voice.[27]

_____ 9. **These words connect the worshipper with other believers in worship (e.g. using "we" not "I" language). This song would be somewhat awkward if sung alone.**
(No = 0, Somewhat = 5, Yes = 10)

"I" language should be avoided in worship in favor of "we" as much as is practical or possible. It would seem that the proper time for "I" language would be upon one's profession of faith in Jesus Christ. After one has united with the body of Christ, the appropriate pronoun becomes "we," except, perhaps, in confession of sin, or a weekly reaffirmation of faith such as saying the Creed, or in singing a solo anthem. Unfortunately, much modern praise music reflects the individualist worship of the self. In the statistics cited above from Maranatha!'s Praise Chorus Book, recall that while only 16 choruses started with the pronoun "we," while almost twice as many (28) began with "I."

Remember that many individualist songs can be rescued by making appropriate changes in the pronouns. Our congregation often closes evening worship with Laurie Klein's "*I Love You, Lord,*" which unfortunately bears the singular pronouns. So we changed it from the first person to the second: "*We* love you, Lord, and we lift…,etc."

---

[26] Robert E. Webber, ed. *Twenty Centuries of Christian Worship*, Volume 2 in *The Complete Library of Christian Worship*, (Nashville: Star Song Publishing Group), p. 106.
[27] It is true that a majority of the psalms (76) are in the first person singular "I," most of these by David (54). Yet the great majority of these singular psalms are of the nature of personal testimonies and connected to specific situations which would require the pronoun "I." There is a place in worship for "I" songs, most likely in the form of solos or anthems of a personal testimony nature. But regular congregational singing should reflect the corporate nature of worship by using "we," "our" and "us."

Chapter 3: Evaluating Worship Music (The Words)

_____ **10. These words connect worshippers with God's people in other eras and other cultures (the communion of the saints). (No = 0, Somewhat = 5, Yes = 10)**

Worship music should reflect the best from every age and culture as a continual reminder of the mystical union shared between all believers of all eras. It is a regrettable error to lock oneself into a particular cultural expression in worship whether it be that of eighteenth century Elizabethan hymns, nineteenth century revivalism and sentimentalism, or twenty-first century Praise and Worship. Marva Dawn asks a key question: "How can what we do in worship give the participants a deeper awareness that they are part of the whole people of God throughout space and time?"[28] Referring to more than just worship music, she elaborates:

> The great advantage of hymnbooks is that they convey a sense of the larger church body, united in worship according to the wisdom of all the people together. Using global music, saying the common creeds of the Church and the Lord's Prayer, singing the *Sanctus*, remembering that the Lord's Supper links us to all Christians everywhere, hosting joint worship services with other denominations or congregations of predominantly another race—all of these help to fix in our minds an awareness of being Church together with all the saints.[29]

At issue in this criterion is whether this song reflects only the era and culture to which we are accustomed in worship, or whether this song connects us in some fresh way with God's people of all places and times.

True worship celebrates the covenant nature of the gracious relationship God has initiated with us through Christ. This relationship ultimately leads to profound joy and deep satisfaction, but it is a God-ordered relationship on the basis of the New Covenant established in Jesus Christ. For this reason all Christian worship must be God-centered and Christ-focused. Anything less quickly degenerates into self-worship or worshiping the worship experience. An important question to ask yourself in worship: Are you loving God more than you are loving

---

[28] Dawn, *A Royal "Waste" of Time*, p. 306.
[29] Ibid.

"loving God"? Worship abhors a vacuum. When the God-centered, Christ-focused, weighty content of worship is minimized the worshiper will inevitably drift into praising the praise event (idolatry). Careful selection of true, significant, excellent words to sing about God and to God through Christ help to ensure the integrity of truly Christian worship."

Chapter Four

EVALUATING WORSHIP MUSIC
(PART TWO: THE SONG'S MUSIC)

Since the music is to be the servant of the message, music is considered secondarily in this evaluation tool. I confess that with respect to music, I am a bit out of my element and have had to rely on others for their expertise. And when it comes to evaluating specific songs, it would be important to consult with someone adept in musicology.

_____ **1. This music appropriately matches the tone and message of the words. (No = 0, Somewhat = 10, Yes = 20)**

The point of the music is to assist the message of the song. It should therefore reflect that intention well. As stated earlier, music carries its own message (dissonant, light, somber, energetic, plodding, ponderous, trite, involved, and so forth). The music should be consonant in tone and message with the words of the song. Obviously most time-honored hymns will bear matching music and message. One thinks of the lofty tone of the tune of *"How Great Thou Art"* (Stuart K. Hine). The tune capably captures the feel of greatness which is the theme of the hymn. The simplicity of the lullaby tune of *"Children of the Heavenly Father"* (Berg/Olson) is likewise well suited to the song's theme of child-like trust.

Marva Dawn points out an incongruity between the lyrics and music of Michael W. Smith's setting of the psalm, "O Lord, our Lord, how majestic is your name in all the earth."

> The words are biblical, of course, but the music of the song isn't *majestic*, which, as the dictionaries tell us, means to be very grand, dignified, lofty, stately. Nor does the melody match the original Hebrew adjective which is also defined as great, mighty, noble, princely. This is not a matter of taste—I like the tune—but probably everyone who heard the melody without the words would agree that its timbre is more playful than august, more like frolic than nobility, more suited to penny whistles than to processional banners and kettledrums. No one would call the melody stately; the result of its constant use in churches is that many people, especially youth, no longer know what the word majestic actually means.[30]

_____ **2. This music exhibits excellence in composition and is musically interesting.** (No = 0, Somewhat = 10, Yes = 20)

> This criterion is the musical mirror-image of the same concern for excellence in poetic craftsmanship of the song's words (number five, above). This is not simply a matter of personal taste. "...(M)ost would agree, for example, that a melody of three notes played in the same succession over and over is not musically interesting."[31] A complete description of what comprises musical excellence is beyond the scope of this book. Marva Dawn has a helpful discussion on pages 299-301 of her *A Royal "Waste" of Time*. Suffice it to say that having endured listening to my three children's piano practice over the years, I suspect that many of the banal tunes of their primer books were not examples of excellence in musical craftsmanship and may have been calculated to spur them on to better things.

_____ **3. This music offers a variety from the style usually sung, reminding worshippers of the global nature of the church.** (No = 0, Somewhat = 10, Yes = 20)

> This is the musical counterpart of number 10 above. Singing

---

[30] Ibid., p. 304.
[31] Ibid., p. 299.

someone else's song from another culture may stretch worshippers, but such stretching is a helpful preventative for provincial narrowness and helps to open our hearts to God's work and God's people in other places and times.

_____ 4. This music is singable, not unnecessarily complex, nor pitched too high or too low.
(No = 0, Somewhat = 10, Yes = 20)

An obviously subjective criteria, this is a simple matter of practicality. It is desirous that God's people sing in worship. Yet our culture does not generally teach people to sing. So the music must be singable, able to be quickly learned and repeated. One Sunday morning our organist inadvertently left the transposer set three steps too high, so that every song was pitched above most worshippers' range. I could observe genuine pain on people's faces as they attempted to worship in song (if anything, during morning worship, the transposer should be pitched a step lower to enable morning voices to warm up).

_____ 5. This music would be acceptable to most worshippers (would be offensive to few worshippers).
(No = 0, Somewhat = 10, Yes = 20)

Another matter of practicality, this criterion recognizes that worship is always offered from a particular cultural context and that for worship to be in the "vernacular" it must be offered from that context. Hopefully over time and with deliberate education, that cultural context would appropriate and embrace worship music from other cultures as well. This concern will sometimes be a matter of Christian forbearance as together we learn to "sing to the Lord a new (or old) song."

However, music that is offensive to many should be avoided. Music that is painfully dissonant or that carries unhelpful cultural associations is best omitted, perhaps for another generation, perhaps forever. Even the broad-minded Barry Liesch would draw some kind of line: "I do take the position that music materials are neutral; any style is *theoretically permissible but not necessarily appropriate....*" (emphasis in the original).[32]

---

[32] Liesch, *New*, p. 204.

Remember that if a tune does not fit the song or if it fails somehow in the preceding criteria, it can possibly be changed. Most hymnals include a metrical index of tunes. If two songs follow the same meter they are often interchangeable. Just be sure that the meter actually fits by singing it through first.

CONCLUSION

These guidelines are not intended to be restrictive, only to safeguard the integrity of worship by becoming intentional about worship music. Too often a too prominent place is given to music in worship as the "lifeline to selfhood." This creates unnecessary squabbles and "turf wars" over "my music vs. your music." Songs are selected because "I like it," with little thought to the purpose and intent of song in worship.

Becoming intentional, especially about the message of worship music, will insure that when we, (as Robert Preus said) "sing our doctrine deep into our hearts," that doctrine will be true, God-centered and Christ-focused, and it will truly glorify God as it forms Christian character and fosters Christian community. With this understanding, we can "sing to the Lord a New (Covenant) song."

APPENDIX A:
WORSHIP MUSIC EVALUATION FORM

Song Title: _____
Author/Composer: _____

PART ONE: THE SONG'S WORDS.

PRELIMINARY CONCERNS

_____ 1. These words are biblically true (doctrinally correct) in every way.
        (PASS or FAIL)

_____ 2. These words are distinctively Christian, either Trinitarian or referencing the atoning work of God in Christ (some mention of grace, mercy, redemption, etc.), or both. For example, it would be awkward to sing this song in a Jewish synagogue.
        (O.K. or CAUTION)

A. THIS SONG IS "ABOUT" GOD (God as the subject of worship)

_____ 3. These words' subject is about some aspect of God's character or God's works that is developed in a consequential way.
        (No = 0, Somewhat = 10, Yes = 20)

_____ 4. These words evidence a progression of thought, not merely repetition of thought.
        (No = 0, Somewhat = 5, Yes = 10)

B. THIS SONG IS "TO" GOD (God as the object of worship)

_____ 5. These words are written with excellence and are a fitting offering to present to God.
        (No = 0, Somewhat = 10, Yes = 20)

_____ 6. These words, or a portion of these words, are directed to God and not merely about God.
        (No = 0, Somewhat = 5, Yes = 10)

C. THIS SONG HELPS FORM CHRISTIAN CHARACTER

_____ 7. These words avoid excessive narcissism (self-absorption). They are more about God's work for us (objective) than our work for or feelings about God (subjective).
        (No = 0, Somewhat = 5, Yes = 10)

_____ 8. These words' response of praise, confession, love, etc. (the imperative) is based on relevant and significant truth about God and his works (the indicative).
  (No = 0, Somewhat = 5, Yes = 10)

D. THIS SONG FOSTERS CHRISTIAN COMMUNITY

_____ 9. These words connect the worshipper with other believers in worship (e.g. using "we" not "I" language). This song would be somewhat awkward sung alone.
  (No = 0, Somewhat = 5, Yes = 10)

_____ 10. These words connect worshippers with God's people in other eras and other cultures (the communion of the saints).
  (No = 0, Somewhat = 5, Yes = 10)

PART TWO: THE SONG'S MUSIC.

_____ 1. This music appropriately matches the tone and message of the words.
  (No = 0, Somewhat = 10, Yes = 20)

_____ 2. This music exhibits excellence in composition and is musically interesting.
  (No = 0, Somewhat = 10, Yes = 20)

_____ 3. This music offers a variety from the style usually sung, reminding worshippers of the global nature of the church.
  (No = 0, Somewhat = 10, Yes = 20)

_____ 4. This music is singable, not unnecessarily complex, nor pitched too high or too low.
  (No = 0, Somewhat = 10, Yes = 20)

_____ 5. This music would be acceptable to most worshippers (would be offensive to few worshippers).
  (No = 0, Somewhat = 10, Yes = 20)

NUMERICAL RATING

(Permission granted to reproduce with credit this form for personal or church use. ©2002 Brian V. Janssen)

For Further Reading

D.A. Carson, ed. *Worship By the Book*. Grand Rapids: Zondervan, 2002.

Marva Dawn. *Reaching Out Without Dumbing Down: A Theology of Worship for the Turn-of-the-Century Culture*. Grand Rapids: Eerdmans, 1995.

John L. Frame. *Worship in Spirit and Truth*. Phillipsburg, NJ: P & R Publishing, 1996.

Os Guiness. *Dining with the Devil*. Grand Rapids: Baker, 1993.

Michael Horton. *A Better Way: Rediscovering the Drama of God-Centered Worship*. Grand Rapids: Baker, 2002.

Leonard R. Payton. *Reforming Our Worship Music*. Wheaton, IL: Crossway Books, 2000.

David F. Wells. *No Place for Truth; or, Whatever Happened to Evangelical Theology?* Grand Rapids: Eerdmans, 1993.

_____. *Losing Our Virtue: Why the Church Must Recover Its Moral Vision*. Grand Rapids: Eerdmans, 1998.

Monte E. Wilson, "Church-O-Rama or Corporate Worship" in *The Compromised Church: the Present Evangelical Crisis*, edited by John H. Armstrong. Wheaton, IL: Crossway Books, 1998.

Brian V. Janssen has been pastor of the First Presbyterian (PCA) Church of Hospers, Iowa since 1986. A graduate of Wheaton College and Trinity Evangelical Divinity School, Brian received the Doctor of Ministry degree in 2007 at Covenant Theological Seminary in St. Louis. The focus of his dissertation was on the long-term effects of the Dutch Reformed Cursillo in Northwest Iowa. He has been married to Susanne for over 25 years, and together they have three children: David, Kristin and Jonathan. You can contact him at pastorbvj@gmail.com.

Also by Brian Janssen

Cursillo—Little Courses in Catharsis: A Critique of the Cursillo Movement (Forthcoming) *Churchisfun.com? Renewing Our Vision for the Church* (Forthcoming) *Christ More Excellent: The Better Signs of Jesus*